YOUR KNOWLEDGE HAS VALUE

David Ratajczak

Is Linux a better desktop operating system than Microsoft Windows?

GRIN Publishing

Bibliographic information published by the German National Library:

The German National Library lists this publication in the National Bibliography; detailed bibliographic data are available on the Internet at http://dnb.dnb.de .

Imprint:

Copyright © 2015 GRIN Verlag GmbH
Print and binding: Books on Demand GmbH, Norderstedt Germany
ISBN: 978-3-656-90352-9

This book at GRIN:

http://www.grin.com/en/e-book/292829/is-linux-a-better-desktop-operating-system-than-microsoft-windows

GRIN - Your knowledge has value

Since its foundation in 1998, GRIN has specialized in publishing academic texts by students, college teachers and other academics as e-book and printed book. The website www.grin.com is an ideal platform for presenting term papers, final papers, scientific essays, dissertations and specialist books.

Is Linux a better desktop operating system than Microsoft Windows?

David Ratajczak

Städt. Albert-Schweitzer-
Gymnasium Plettenberg
Facharbeit GK Englisch

Is Linux a better desktop operating system than MS Windows?

I. Introduction

What is Linux?

When we hear the name „Linux" we usually think about an operating system for nerds and other people with too much free time. Well, that's only partially true since Linux itself isn't an operating system. Linux is a core for operating systems which are built around it[1].

Yet all Linux based operating system are very similar in use and are all referred to as „Linux" - even though the correct term for these systems would be „GNU/Linux" (while, as already mentioned, only the core itself is called Linux) because they are all released under the GNU Public License[2].

The history of Linux dates back to the early nineties when Linus Torvalds, a student of computer science and a member of the Swedish minority of Finland started to write his own little operating system core just for fun.
Later he mentioned this operating system core on a newsgroup and he also added the possibility of releasing it under the GPL – eventually he did so.

The early nineties were also the era of the early Internet and people all over the world showed interest in Linux and it quickly progressed. Due to the open nature of the GPL everyone could download the source code of Linux and add, remove, fix or improve things. More and more developers gathered. Linux "Distributions" - the various operating systems based on Linux – created and spread throughout the Internet[3]. Today big computer companies such as Hewlett Packard or Intel have paid employees who contribute to Linux because these companies rely on Linux based technologies so every progress in the Linux world is in their very own interest[4][5].

---

[1] "Linux", 16 February 2015, http://en.wikipedia.org/wiki/Linux
[2] "Linux", 16 February 2015, http://en.wikipedia.org/wiki/Linux
[3] Dave Hayward, The history of Linux", http://www.techradar.com/news/software/operating-systems/the-history-of-linux-how-time-has-shaped-the-penguin-1113914
[4] „Debian Partners", 16 February 2015, https://www.debian.org/partners/
[5] "Linus Torvalds defends his right to shame Linux kernel developers", 16 February 2015, http://arstechnica.com/information-technology/2013/07/linus-torvalds-defends-his-right-to-shame-linux-kernel-developers/

Where do we encounter it?

Today, around 25 years later, Linux basically runs the modern world. It's everywhere.

When you fire up your computer's Internet browser and connect to a website this website is most likely run on a Linux server[6]. All the big services, such as Facebook or Google heavily rely on Linux[78].

If you go to an electronics store and buy one of these fancy and new mobile phones with Android or Tizen – well, you've just bought a little computer running Linux because both, Tizen and Android are based on Linux[910].

Look around your living room. Do you have a device to watch DVD's[11]? A device to record TV shows to a hard drive[12] or a little media center computer which you use to stream MP3's and movies from your PC or laptop[13]? Do you have a modern TV which allows you to browse and open media files from your pen drives or even has the ability to access the Internet in order to show you the news or the newest videos from Youtube[14]? Congratulations, there's a big chance that these devices run Linux based software.

But that's not the end. Linux can also be a part of security mechanisms[15], medical devices or even run the war ships of the US Navy[16]. But you can also run one of the many Linux distributions on your computer which you use at home or at work. In fact there's *nothing* Linux couldn't do or run or be a part of.

---

[6] "Usage share of operating systems", 16 February 2015,
http://en.wikipedia.org/wiki/Usage_share_of_operating_systems
[7] "How Does Facebook Work? The Nuts and Bolts [Technology Explained]", 16 February 2015,
http://www.makeuseof.com/tag/facebook-work-nuts-bolts-technology-explained/
[8] „How Google uses Linux", 16 February 2015, http://lwn.net/Articles/357658/
[9] "Tizen", 16 February 2015, http://en.wikipedia.org/wiki/Tizen
[10] "Android is Based on Linux, But What Does That Mean?", 16 February 2015,
http://www.howtogeek.com/189036/android-is-based-on-linux-but-what-does-that-mean/
[11] „Toshiba HD-A1 Review", 16 February 2015, http://www.ign.com/articles/2006/06/03/toshiba-hd-a1-review
[12] „VDR", 16 February 2015, http://wiki.ubuntuusers.de/VDR
[13] „Linux als Home Entertainment Server mit UPnP und DLNA", 16 February 2015, http://www.linux-magazin.de/Ausgaben/2013/01/Videostreaming
[14] „So hacken Sie Ihr Smart-TV", 16 February 2015, http://www.pcwelt.de/ratgeber/So-hacken-Sie-Ihren-Smart-TV-5899304.html
[15] 16 February 2015, http://www.zoneminder.com/
[16] "The Navy's newest warship is powered by Linux", 16 February 2015, http://arstechnica.com/information-technology/2013/10/the-navys-newest-warship-is-powered-by-linux/

What makes it special?

Linux operating systems are very special because everyone around the world can contribute to them. You can download the source code[17] to your computer and, as already mentioned, edit it. This way Linux basically belongs to everyone – or better said: everyone can adapt it and the distributions around it to fit his needs. This way Linux is extremely adaptable and can run on a wide range of hardware because everyone can also add his own hardware drivers to the core.

That's also the reason why Linux is so wide spread. Only because Linux is available to everyone it could be adapted to your desktop computer, your TV, your mobile phone or your war ship – if you have any. It's so adaptable that there's only a minority of the top 500 super computers which does not run Linux.

This special concept enabled Linux to conquer our modern world. It's nearly everywhere and we won't get rid of it for the next decades to come.

---

[17] kernel.org, 16 February 2015, https://www.kernel.org/

And what exactly is Linux Mint?

In the Linux world there are hundreds of Linux distributions who are constantly improved, updated or released. These distributions target different audiences such as developers, server administrators, hackers, children, or normal end users.

Fig. 1: The standard desktop of Linux Mint 17

Linux Mint is a distribution of Linux which targets normal end users. It provides a traditional user interface which is called Cinnamon. Additionally there are other "flavors" of Linux Mint which provide similar user interfaces which target high end computer (such as KDE) or low end computers (such as XFCE or Mate)[18].

For this essay I have chosen Linux Mint because of the traditional user interface it features and because it targets the normal end user who only wants to finish some office work, browse Facebook, play some arcade game, and listen to his extensive collection of illegally obtained MP3's.

Today Linux Mint is regarded as one of the 'easier' distributions of Linux because the operating system tries to not bother the user with anything complicated to set up or install. Using Linux Mint also provides a rather similar experience to using Windows 7.

That's the second reason why I have chosen Linux Mint for this essay. Windows 7 and Linux Mint both provide a traditional yet not archaic desktop experience. For example it would be unfair to compare Linux Mint to Windows 95 or compare Arch Linux (a distribution which targets Linux professionals and enthusiasts)[19] to Windows 8.1 simply because these systems are either too modern, too different or too chronologically distant from each other. Windows 8/8.1, for example, added features to the user interface[20] which we might never see in a Linux OS.

---

[18] Linux Mint Homepage, 16 February, http://www.linuxmint.com/
[19] Arch Linux Homepage, 16 February, https://www.archlinux.org/
[20] "Windows 8 Metro UI: A Bold New Face for Windows", 16 February 2015,
http://www.pcworld.com/article/251340/windows_8_metro_ui_a_bold_new_face_for_windows.html

And since I will use this essay to check if Linux is a better desktop operating system than Microsoft Windows the two competitors, Linux Mint and Windows 7, simply provide a fair comparison.

II. Technical Aspects

Installing the operating system

The installation of both, Windows 7 and Linux, is fairly easy as both operating systems provide a graphical installer which guides you through the process of the installation and can be controlled with computer mouse. In fact all you need to do is to burn a DVD with the respective operating system, open your computer's disc tray, put in the disc and restart the computer. Yet there are still differences.

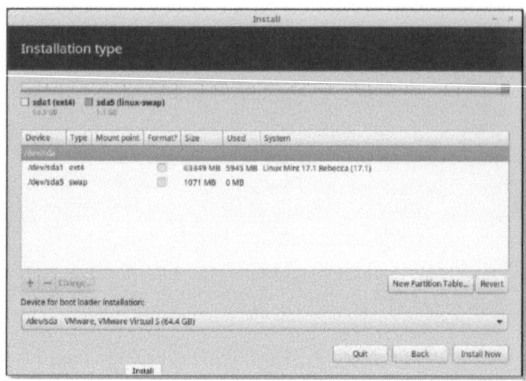

Fig. 2 The graphical installer of Linux Mint

One big difference between Linux Mint 17 and Windows 7 is that Linux Mint 17 can boot

into a "live environment" where you can try the operating system before installing it. If you don't like it you can simply turn off your computer and remove the disc. If Linux Mint appeals to you, you can just double click an icon on Mint's desktop which will start the graphical installer. Windows 7, on the other hand, gives you no such option. A Windows 7 DVD will boot directly into its installer.

Fig. 3 Linux Mint's "Live Environment"

Both installers basically do the same thing. You will be asked to choose on which partition you want to install your operating systems. Additionally both installers enable you to create or delete partitions if necessary. You will also be asked to choose your display language and keyboard layout, your current time zone and to provide a username and a password which you will use to log in to your system later.

Since the rest is completely automated once you did the things mentioned above there's nothing more to mention. The only big difference between installing Linux Mint 17 and Windows 7 is Mint's live mode which, as already said, enables you to test it before you install it.

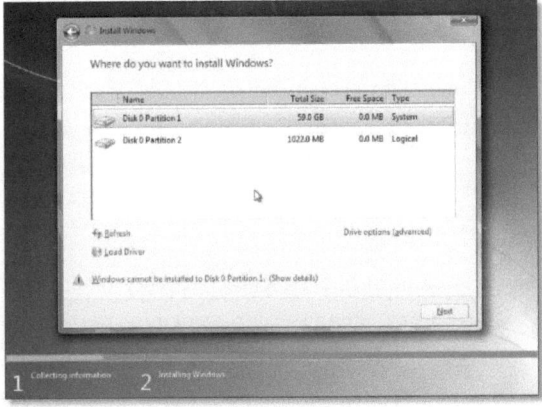

Fig. 4 The installer of Windows 7

Hardware Drivers

Every operating system needs drivers. Basically drivers are little programs which allow your operating system to communicate with your computer's hardware. For example you need drivers for your graphical processing unit (GPU), your WIFI adapter and many other pieces of hardware.

Linux in general and Windows are very different at handling drivers. Most drivers you'll ever need are already inside the Linux Kernel. This way your computer is ready once Linux is installed. The only exception is when you have exotic hardware or when you want closed-source drivers for some piece of hardware, e.g. a GPU.

Windows, on the other hand, only comes with the most necessary drivers for basic network and videos tasks. In order to use your displays native resolution, your WIFI device and your computer's full performance you need to install a number of drivers from your hardware's manufacturer. These can be found on CD's which often come with hardware you buy or obtained on the Internet.

Linux Mint is quite convenient when it's about hardware drivers. As all drivers you need are already inside the Linux Kernel, it should run, as mentioned above, out of the box. In case you want or need additional drivers the operating system has a simple program for that which gives you the option to view and install all available additional drivers for your hardware.

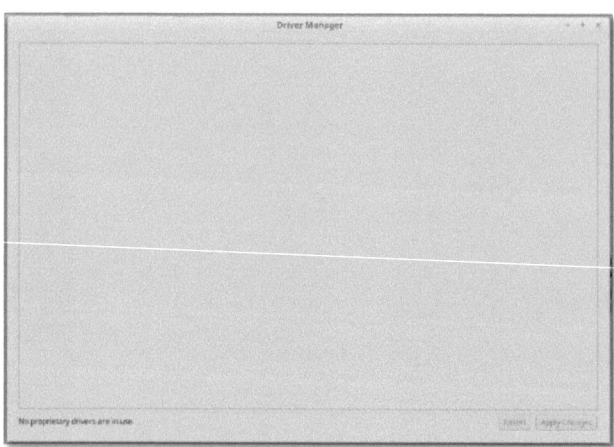

Fig. 5 Mint's driver tool. In this case it hasn't found any additional drivers because all needed ones are already inside Linux

Your computer's performance and resource consumption

Modern computers are very complicated machines and so are the programs which run on them. The way programs are written can have a huge impact on how your computer performs. If a programmer has many bad programming habits his program may consume more resources than it has to which results in a generally lower performance of your computer.

Fig. 6 performance of Linux Mint 17

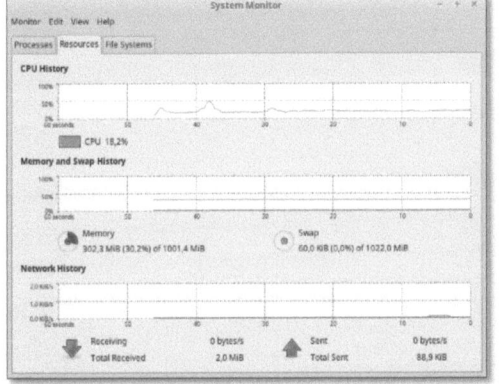

Both, Windows 7 and Linux Mint 17, come with a set of preinstalled applications and services while still having to run themselves. You can compare how well both systems perform compared to each other by starting them while they are still freshly installed. Now you can just go ahead and check how much RAM (Random Access Memory) and CPU power (Central Processing Unit; processor) they consume.

Fig. 7 performance of Windows 7

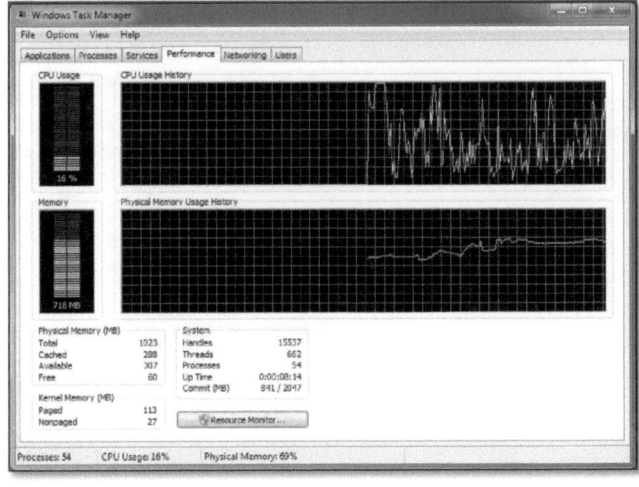

In figure 6 and 7 we can see that Linux Mint 17 outperforms Windows 7 on the same (virtual) hardware. Linux Mint's CPU usage stays nearly constantly at 16% while Windows 7's CPU usage fluctuates between ~20% and 80-90%.

And while a freshly installed Linux Mint 17 consumes around 300 Megabytes of RAM

Windows 7 consumes more than 650 Megabytes of memory.

Both systems have no additional software installed and both systems have their standard configuration. You can clearly see that Linux Mint 17 outperforms Windows 7. Yet I have to add that both operating systems run on virtual machines created with a program called VMware. The results of this test could look quite different on real computers.

III. Everyday use

Accessing your programs and files

In order for you to work efficiently with your computer you need the ability to quickly access the documents and programs you need to get your tasks done. Many recent operating systems have quite interesting concepts for doing so. Yet Linux Mint and Windows 7 keep the traditional approach.

Fig. 8 The standard Windows 7 desktop

Both operating systems feature a classic desktop on which you can place icons which represent your programs or documents. They also both feature a large horizontal and configurable bar at the bottom of your screen with a menu in the lower left corner which gives you access to all your programs. It also shows some quick launch icons which can instantly start a

Fig. 9 The standard Linux Mint 17 desktop

program and a small area which displays some general information about your system.

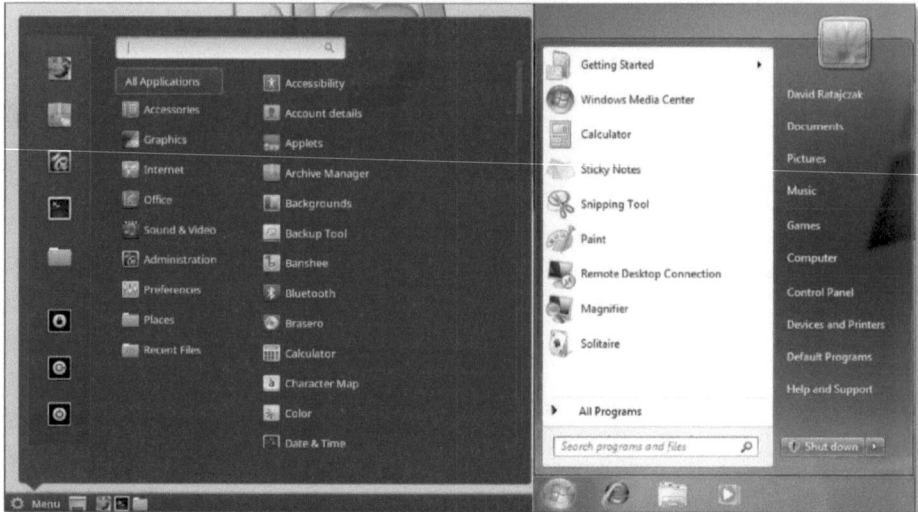

Fig. 10 The menus in direct comparison

The real difference lies in the menus in the lower left corner. As you can see Mint's menu is much larger and it sorts your programs into categories such as "Office" or "Administration". It also displays some application icons set as favorites on the left side of the menu.

On the other hand Windows 7's menu has a large white area in which your most used programs are displayed. You can add favorites, too. On the right side you'll find links to some places on your hard drive and system settings. When you click on "All Programs" you will find all installed programs in folders named after their developing companies.

All in all I think that Mint's concept is much better because it gives you a good old traditional desktop and a quick way to find the application you need without having to pin it your task bar or desktop. If you want to start a program your rarely use on Windows 7 you have to find it in your menus, use the search function or add it to your desktop. In case you have many programs your desktop can fill up quite quickly. That's the reason why I think Linux Mint 17 gives you a much better solution.

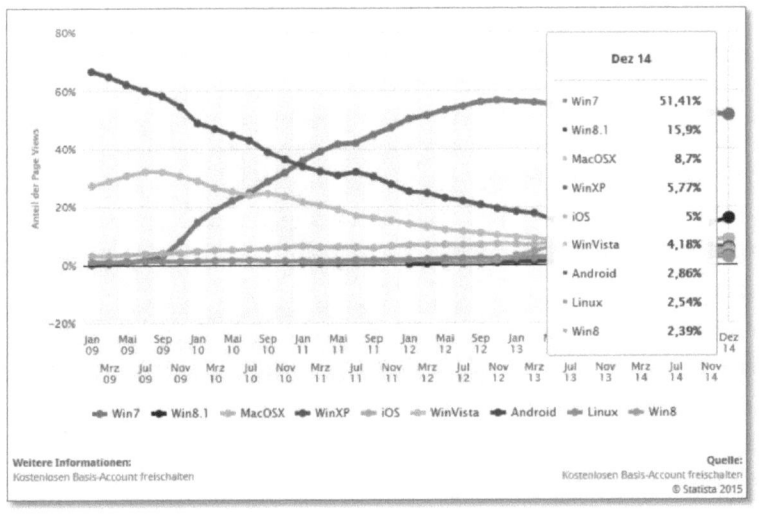

Dez 14	
• Win7	51,41%
• Win8.1	15,9%
• MacOSX	8,7%
• WinXP	5,77%
• iOS	5%
• WinVista	4,18%
• Android	2,86%
• Linux	2,54%
• Win8	2,39%

Fig. 11 computer operating system, '09 - '15; source: Statista

These days criminals are present on the Internet, too. They can steal money from your bank account, change your profile picture on Facebook or infect your computer with harmful malicious software called computer viruses.

This way there's constant need for software which prevents such criminal acts. Windows 7 has a market share of over 50%. This makes it the most popular operating system and the most popular target for attackers. This means that you need security software to stay secure. As you can see, Linux has a much smaller market share of around ~2.5%[21]. We already know that there is a really large number of Linux distributions of which Linux Mint is just a single one, too. It's just one among many. This fact makes it more secure than Windows 7 because it has a really small market share and no one is really interested in finding big security flaws. There are virtually no viruses which can target Linux, especially Linux Mint. You can run it without security software and don't have to worry about it. If Linux had a much larger market share in the future it would change, of course.

---

[21] "Marktanteile der führenden Betriebssystemversionen in Deutschland von Januar 2009 bis Januar 2015", February 2015, http://de.statista.com/statistik/daten/studie/158102/umfrage/marktanteile-von-betriebssystemen-in-deutschland-seit-2009/

Using a computer for entertainment is a very important aspect for computer users these days. People watch films, listen to music and play videogames.

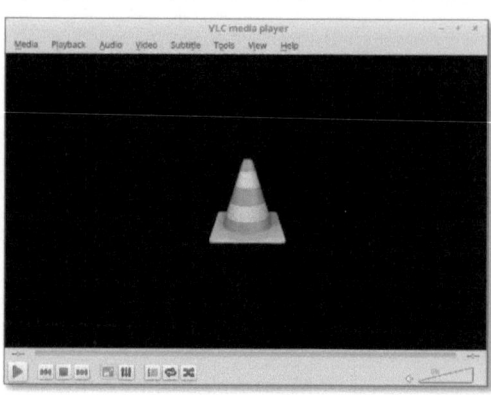

Fig. 12 "VLC Player" on Linux Mint

Both operating systems come with a set of multimedia applications which allow you watch or films and listen to music. Windows 7 comes with the "Windows Media Player" which allows you to open a number of audio and video formats and organize your media in a library. On Linux Mint "Banshee" and "VLC Player" are preinstalled. "Banshee" organizes and plays your music while "VLC Player" can open all relevant video formats[22].

Even though a standard Linux Mint 17 can open some more files than a standard Windows 7 there's no big difference which should be mentioned.

Gaming, on the other hand, is a different topic. Due to the low market share of Linux many game developers don't program their games for it because they cannot expect much profit from it. Because of this there are only few top notch games available for Linux, even though there are more and more as the trend is changing[23]. Additionally you can use software such as "WINE" in order to run Windows games and other software on Linux – even though it's not always reliable[24].

[22] „Windows Media Player oder VLC?", 16 February 2015, http://www.pc-magazin.de/ratgeber/windows-media-player-oder-vlc-player-2111897.html

[23] "Steam's Linux game count explodes in one year, big publishers still absent", 16 February 2016 http://www.pcworld.com/article/2098972/steams-linux-game-count-explodes-in-one-year-big-publishers-still-absent.html

[24] WINE Homepage, 16 February, https://www.winehq.org/

Office Work

Office workers need to work with spreadsheets, text documents, databases, and presentations. On the software market you'll find a vast number of products for these tasks.

Linux Mint comes with preinstalled and complete office suite called "LibreOffice" which can do

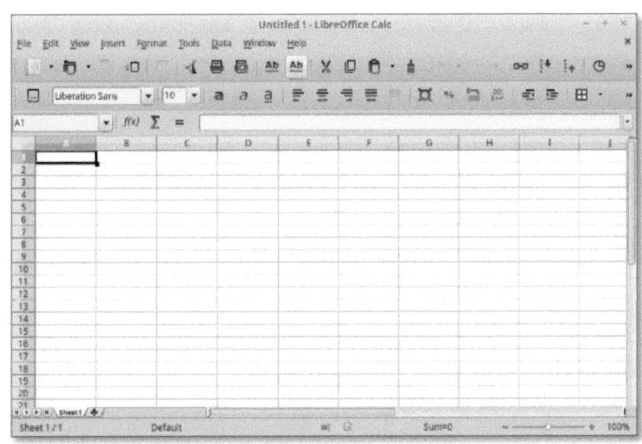

Fig. 13 The spreadsheet module of "LibreOffice" on Mint

all of the things mentioned above. It even has a high compatibility with Microsoft's office formats.

Windows 7 doesn't have any preinstalled office suite. A basic Windows 7 installation only has a small program called "Wordpad" which can handle some text documents. If you want to do office work you have to download a free office suite such as "OpenOffice" or "LibreOffice" or buy a license for Microsoft's office products.

This is an advantage of Linux Mint because you can install it and instantly start to work.

Installing additional software

Many people need their computers for many other tasks than just office work or multimedia. Computers are also used by engineers, artists, musicians, teachers and kids. This is where additional software comes into play.

If you want to use additional software on Windows 7 you have to download it from the Internet, which can be a rather unsecure source[25]. You can also buy software on CD's and DVD's which you put into your disc drive.

Linux, especially Linux Mint, gives you completely different approach. The software for Linux Mint is stored in repositories on the Internet which can be accessed

Fig. 14 Linux Mint's software managing program

with Mint's "Software Manager". The programs from this source are secure and you don't have to worry about installing any kind of malicious software. If you don't find the software you need with the "Software Manager" you can search the Internet. Many developers offer Linux installer packages for Mint but this comes with the same risk as downloading programs for Windows.

---

[25] "How does a computer get infected with a virus or spyware?", 16 February 2015, http://www.computerhope.com/issues/ch001045.htm

Networking

In our time a connection to the Internet is extremely important because we use the Internet for a wide range of tasks. Luckily both, Linux Mint 17 and Windows 7, are easily connectable to the Internet.

On both systems you just plug in your network cable and you will instantly be connected to the Internet (through your local network). If you plug in a WIFI device both systems will display a list of available WIFI networks. You can simply enter your PSK and surf the Internet.

IV. Conclusion

In conclusion I think that both operating systems are equivalent to each other. Yet both systems have their specific pros and cons. We saw that Linux Mint is more secure than Windows 7 because it has a small market share. And because it has a small market share many programming companies don't target it. Windows 7 might have a bigger number of available programs, yet you need more time to start working after installing it.

V. Literaturverzeichnis

Hinweis: Die Screenshots der benutzen Webseiten befinden sich auf der beigelegten DVD im Verzeichnis „Fußnoten"! Die Dateinamen entsprechen den Nummern der Fußnoten.

"Linux", 16 February 2015, http://en.wikipedia.org/wiki/Linux
"Linux", 16 February 2015, http://en.wikipedia.org/wiki/Linux
Dave Hayward, The history of Linux", http://www.techradar.com/news/software/operating-systems/the-history-of-linux-how-time-has-shaped-the-penguin-1113914
"Debian Partners", 16 February 2015, https://www.debian.org/partners/
"Linus Torvalds defends his right to shame Linux kernel developers", 16 February 2015, http://arstechnica.com/information-technology/2013/07/linus-torvalds-defends-his-right-to-shame-linux-kernel-developers/
"Usage share of operating systems", 16 February 2015, http://en.wikipedia.org/wiki/Usage_share_of_operating_systems
"How Does Facebook Work? The Nuts and Bolts [Technology Explained]", 16 February 2015, http://www.makeuseof.com/tag/facebook-work-nuts-bolts-technology-explained/
How Google uses Linux", 16 February 2015, http://lwn.net/Articles/357658/
"Tizen", 16 February 2015, http://en.wikipedia.org/wiki/Tizen
"Android is Based on Linux, But What Does That Mean?", 16 February 2015, http://www.howtogeek.com/189036/android-is-based-on-linux-but-what-does-that-mean/
„Toshiba HD-A1 Review", 16 February 2015, http://www.ign.com/articles/2006/06/03/toshiba-hd-a1-review
„VDR", 16 February 2015, http://wiki.ubuntuusers.de/VDR
„Linux als Home Entertainment Server mit UPnP und DLNA", 16 February 2015, http://www.linux-magazin.de/Ausgaben/2013/01/Videostreaming
„So hacken Sie Ihr Smart-TV", 16 February 2015, http://www.pcwelt.de/ratgeber/So-hacken-Sie-Ihren-Smart-TV-5899304.html
16 February 2015, http://www.zoneminder.com/
"The Navy's newest warship is powered by Linux", 16 February 2015, http://arstechnica.com/information-technology/2013/10/the-navys-newest-warship-is-powered-by-linux/
kernel.org, 16 February 2015, https://www.kernel.org/
Linux Mint Homepage, 16 February, http://www.linuxmint.com/
Arch Linux Homepage, 16 February, https://www.archlinux.org/
"Windows 8 Metro UI: A Bold New Face for Windows", 16 February 2015, http://www.pcworld.com/article/251340/windows_8_metro_ui_a_bold_new_face_for_windows.html

"Marktanteile der führenden Betriebssystemversionen in Deutschland von Januar 2009 bis Januar 2015", February 2015, http://de.statista.com/statistik/daten/studie/158102/umfrage/marktanteile-von-betriebssystemen-in-deutschland-seit-2009/

„Windows Media Player oder VLC?", 16 February 2015, http://www.pc-magazin.de/ratgeber/windows-media-player-oder-vlc-player-2111897.html

"Steam's Linux game count explodes in one year, big publishers still absent", 16 February 2016 http://www.pcworld.com/article/2098972/steams-linux-game-count-explodes-in-one-year-big-publishers-still-absent.html

WINE Homepage, 16 February, https://www.winehq.org/

"How does a computer get infected with a virus or spyware?", 16 February 2015, http://www.computerhope.com/issues/ch001045.htm